Tina,

Même si ce séjour à Lyon fut de courte durée, j'espère que tu auras pu apprécier ton séjour et perfectionner ton français.

Ce livre te permettra d'avoir un souvenir de Lyon.

Bonne chance et sans doute à bientôt !

Christophe

Tina,

Bonne chance pour la suite.

A bientôt j'espère,

bertrand.

Chère Tina,

C'était un plaisir de t'avoir avec nous ! J'espère que tu as pu voir au moins quelques "couleurs" de Lyon...

Plein de bonnes choses,

Anna

Tina,

Ce séjour fut très bref, mais suffisamment long toutefois j'espère, pour te donner envie de revenir très prochainement. Ravie d'avoir pu faire plus ample connaissance avec toi le week-end dernier, sache que notre maison te sera toujours ouverte. Donnes-nous de tes nouvelles et à bientôt !

Take care !   Christine

Hello,

I know that I should not write to you in English but you know... I am sure that when you come back to France, soon I hope, I will be too busy that during the past month and that we will be able to take you around (with my husband of course)

Kind regards and see you soon,

Sandrine

Chère Tina,

J'espère que ce petit séjour linguistique en France et de découvert de l'entreprise Merck Lipha t'aidera pour le futur.

Bonne chance, Tina, et peut-être le plaisir de te revoir sur Lyon.

Marie

Louis Jacquemin

Colors of Lyon

EDITIONS
LA TAILLANDERIE

Collection directed by Gérald Gambier
Layouts Laurent Grasset
Translated into English by Christopher Kilgallon

Photographs

Vincent Arnaud : pages 4, 5, 6, 7, 8, 9, 11, 12, 13, 14, 16, 17, 18, 19, 20, 22, 23, 25, 26, 27, 30, 36, 37, 38, 39, 40, 41, 42, 43, 44, 50, 51, 52, 57, 58, 62, 63, 64, 65, 66, 67, 68, 71, 72, 73, 76, 79, 82, 85h, 86, 89, 90, 91, 92, 93, 94, 95, 98, 99, 101, 102, 108, 112, 114, 116, 117, 118, 120, 125.

Gérald Gambier : cover. Pages 10, 21, 24, 28, 29, 31, 33, 35, 46, 49, 60, 61, 75, 77, 85b, 87, 88, 97, 104, 107, 109, 110, 113, 119, 121, 122, 123, 124, 126, 127.

Delphine Manin : page 3.

Annick Sintes : page 83.

© Editions la Taillanderie
rue des frères Lumière
01400 Châtillon-sur-Chalaronne

ISBN 2-87629-181-9 anglais
ISSN 1243-4388

The Colours of Lyon

I - The Colours of Lyon

From the Croix-Rousse, one can see the whole of the "Presqu'île".

The city of Lyon originated on the side of the Croix-Rousse plateau where Ségusiaves Gauls lived as long ago as 500 years before Christ, and on the top of the Fourvière hill, where the Romans were to settle in 43 B.C.

Over time, the two primitive populations intermingled and thrived.

Already, at the dawn of Lugdunum (the Latin name for Lyon), the Rhône courted the Saône, caressed it with its numerous branches at the foot of the two hills, and was to triumph over it further to the south, before heading off to the Mediterranean sunshine.

Little by little, the city was to spread out around its two silver-green rivers with, before being dedicated to the crimson-coloured Beaujolais much later.

The "Canuts" hill.

A great Eastward-bound route.

Place Bellecour, colours and shade, coolness !

Today, Lyon extends well beyond the Rhône and its main tributary; from the "northern confines of the Croix-Rousse" up to its industrial neighbors in Oullins, La Mulatière, Saint-Fons, Vénissieux, and from its Saint-Rambert and Saint-Just districts up to the city of Villeurbanne. Some five-hundred thousand people now live in this area.

The sun visits our city in a somewhat parsimonious or lazy manner; it often appears in the soft down of clouds or behind the dark crêpe of stormy skies.

Nonetheless, from the quays, one is overwhelmed by the colours of Lyon.

A garden in the "Bellecour" square.

The bronze horse.

The Saône and its quaysides, splashes of light under stormy blue clouds.

The silvery Saône.

Notre-Dame de Fourvière, Lyon's acropolis and second basilica.

Near the amphithéâtre, lawns and flowerbeds in the "Jardin des Plantes".

Statues on the bridges admire themselves in the mirror of the Rhône.

The external walls are reflected in the Saône's green mirror or in the Rhône's silvery glimmer. The buildings climb the slopes or line up behind the rows of plane trees. For the past couple of decades, efforts have been made to clean them: the ochre, pink or cream-coloured tones often stand out against the white surroundings. The red roofs and the more staid opening of the streets create a kind of harmony in this city which reminds one of Florence or Pisa and the banks of the Arno. But the quays of our Florentine or Pisa neighbors are not as shaded as ours.

The city has numerous parks and open spaces.

- "Not enough!" lament the ecologists, quite rightly, enamored as they are of clean 3air and chlorophyll.

- "The areas which can be developed are not infinite, and it costs a lot of money to transform them!" reply the authorities, fortunately concerned with how public funds are spent.

The Notre-Dame de Fourvière basilica and its four towers, the bell-tower of the old chapel and the metal tower are the most well-known structures in Lyon. These three timeless monuments emerge from the dense garden foliage of the Rosaire. The city has provided them with a new youth. Decaying trees have been replaced; red-sand lanes run between the thickets that blossom every spring.

Beyond the tower that many Lyon residents wrongly attribute to Eiffel - are they jealous of Parisians? - a path runs along the crest of the hill and over the viaduct on which there was once a tramway whose role was to take the dead and those who lamented them to the Loyasse cemetery. This

In the Tête-d'or park, where rowing along a silver ribbon is one of many pleasures to be enjoyed.

What remains of the monastery

Previous page :
L'île Barbe, a peaceful haven where
Charlemagne wanted to sleep his last sleep.

path enables one to admire the Croix-Rousse; it overlooks a vast prairie where, a few decades ago, cattle and sheep still grazed.

Above the Saône, on its left bank, in front of the former École de Tissage (Weaving School), which has since become the Diderot lycée, along the Place Rouville, and at the foot of the famous Brunet house with its 365 windows, like the number of days in a year, and its four entrances, like the number of seasons, runs the trim little Jardin des Chartreux. Between the trees, the view overlooks the quays beyond the roofs of the buildings. The light-green ribbon of the river guides one's glance to the city's bell-towers and domes; the paths in this park wind in and out between the flowery thickets, the tulip, pansy or rhododendron flower-beds where several lovely monuments have been erected. Those created by Pierre Dupont, Xavier Privat, or Salendre's "Le Printemps" are amongst the most famous.

The most famous garden of all.

Previous double page spread :
The Saône winding its way between the Croix-Rousse and Fourvière.

The Tête-d'or park,
opened during the XIXth century,
gateway.

A boat called Le Rhône *on the Saône.*

All our compatriots and our visitors are familiar with the Place Bellecour and its "bronze horse" with Louis XIV sitting astride it, sculpted by Lemot as a Roman emperor, and whose pedestal is decorated with the Rhône and Saône sculpted by the Coustou brothers. In his youth, the future great king, passing through Lyon with his mother and Mazarin "uttered sweet nothings" to Marie Mancini in Bellecour. The 18th century lime trees have been replaced by chestnut trees. Fountains of water gush forth in blue basins near kiosks where dazzling, multicoloured flowers are sold.

Since we are going to speak about colours in this book, how can we not speak of those in the Tête d'Or park? Legend has it that a head of Christ made of precious metal was buried in this area! Under the Second Empire, the Prefect Vaïsse opened up the grand thoroughfares which crossed the city from north to south. But, in addition, he wanted to create a large park extending over a hundred hectares. The Bühler brothers drew up plans in the English style. Around the lake where swans glide, the lanes seem to run between magnificent trees and wind around vast lawns, flower beds and spots of variegated colours which are tastefully maintained by the gar-

The Rhône : the king of rivers hastes towards its union with the Saône.

deners. At the height of the season, there is a rose-garden which includes more than fifty thousand roses; they grow just next to the mauve-coloured irises, along with rows of tulips, like surprising rainbows, with gold-coloured pansies, the red or blue globes of the hydrangeas.

The artist's palette tries to do justice to the sunset on the lake, or the pastel colours which are diffused by autumn mists under the trees. In memory's island, the War Memorial by Jean and Auguste Larrivé is dominated by pall-bearers carrying a casket up to the sky. In the winter fog, this cenotaph takes on a heroic aspect: the soul of war victims appears in order to conquer a blissful eternity!

Apart from these immense collections of colours, the city has numerous parks and open spaces: among others, we should mention the wide avenues or boulevards shaded by plane trees, the garden which is like a jewel-case for the Trois Gaules amphitheater; the Place Sathonay recently redecorated so tastefully, the Place des Célestins, its ornamental lake and its magnolias with their glossy leaves, the archaeological garden near the white cathedral, and, beyond the Rhône, the Place Morand or the Prefecture area and up to the modern Parilly Park...

Between the place Bellecour and the river Rhône, the new Antonin Poncet square.

The Blood Stained Years:
177 / 202 A.D

II - The Blood-Stained Years:
177 - 202 A.D.

Amphitheatre of the martyrs of the year 177.
Next page : near the ancient necropolis, Saint-Just's cross.

After the death of Christ, his followers, persecuted by the Roman occupants and by Jews who collaborated with them, emigrated. During the 1st century, they reached Phyrgia (in the north-east of modern-day Turkey); then, little by little, they went by boat to Gaul, and via the Rhône, to Lugdunum.

This is why, as of the 2nd century, there was already a Christian community in the town.

On the other hand, along with these Christians came adepts of the goddess Cybele and her son Attis. The latter died during the winter; in the spring, his mother brought him back to life. Both were believed to be responsible for abundant harvests, good health and the well-being of the faithful. The cult of Cybele was a bloody one: all her adepts had to undergo an initiation ritual involving blood from a bull with which they anointed their bodies. The

Saint-Jean.

Romans were reasonably tolerant as regarded new religions, as long as the adepts were willing to pay homage to the emperors. In this way, they managed to subjugate the vanquished peoples even more.

With these first Christians from Lugdunum came Saint Pothin. He was a disciple of Polycarp of Smyrna who himself had followed Jean the Evangelist, author of the Apocalypse. Where did these emigrants live? No one can be absolutely certain. The less adventurous ones had to spread out between the Saône and the branches of the Rhône in the Canabae isles (the modern-day Presqu'île), but others were to reach the Roman city on the summit of the hill which crowned the Forum, the theaters and the temple of Cybele. Almost everyone spoke Greek; Epagathus was a dignitary, Alexander a doctor; Sanctus, a deacon; Blandine, a young slave; Pontique just a lad of fifteen!

What caused the persecution of 177 A.D.?

The followers of Cybele had celebrated the initiation of neophytes in the religion which they felt was the true one. On the morrow, the Lugdunum Christians gathered to mediate on Holy Friday whilst awaiting to celebrate the Resurrection of Christ. Amable Audin (1) pointed out that the pagan festival was on March 28th that year and the Christian Easter on the 31st. As the young Lugdunum congregation was not very numerous, their opponents unleashed their fury on them.

The Christians were then assailed: they were accused of the worst horrors: cannibalism, since they claimed to eat the body of Christ and drink his blood; incest, since they claimed to love all men as brothers; treason, since they refused to pay homage to the emperors; sacrilege, since they scorned the

Roman countryside ? See the acqueducts in Lugdunum.

The oldest church still open to worshippers (XIVth century),
the Saint-Martin d'Ainay basilica.
Previous page : little Blandine, suffered martyrdom despite her young age.

sacrifice of Cybele's bull and being bathed in the blood of this animal whose genitals were burnt in order to offer them up "spiritually" to the goddess!

The authorities handed all those who were arrested over to torturers. The old bishop Pothin, in spite of his 90 years, was kicked and struck; he was bludgeoned and stoned: he died two years later in a prison, where - we read in the letter of the Christians to their brothers in Phyrgia - the poor prisoners were so numerous that many died of asphyxiation.

The emperor Marcus Aurelius, who was nonetheless a philosopher, asked about the fate reserved for the Christians, issued an order to arrest those who were accused, then to torture them and release those who were willing to make a sacrifice to the gods of Rome.

All those who were Roman citizens and who affirmed their faith were beheaded; the others underwent the most atrocious forms of torture, such as those suffered by the young slave Blandine whose courage and resistance left his torturers dumbfounded. Running out of imagination and sadistic tactics, they finally wrapped him up in a net that they fastened to the horns of an enraged bull!

However after this persecution, the Church of Lyon prospered. Saint Augustin rightly pointed out: "The blood of martyrs breeds eternity".

Irenaeus, the second Bishop of Lyon, was absent from the city when these horrors took place. He died during another persecution in 202, during which more than 19 000 other Christians were to die, having declared their religious beliefs. This is only a legend, but an extraordinarily moving one!

Many legends arose during the centuries which followed these terrible events. However firm one's faith may be, it can be enriched by glorious images born of the imagination!

One legend is due to the crypt of the Chapel de l'Antiquaille. This name still remains that of a hospital located at the top of the Chemin Neuf hill. The name, Antiquaille (meaning "Antiquities", was applied to a 16th-century house where Pierre Salla, a rich citizen of Lyon and master of the stables of Charles VIII, grouped together all scattered remains

The grand theatre in Lugdunum.

of the Roman monuments. In the 17th century, this house devolved upon the religious community of the Visitation, whose Mother Superior was Madame de Rians. The latter claimed to have had a vision of God during her sleep; He revealed to her that, in the ground under the chapel, there was the prison of the tormented martyrs. Thus, one began to dig and soon, several natural cavities were discovered, such as those found in caves around Lyon. One was very narrow and seemed to take the shape of a kind of small bench. The pious lady was convinced. Henceforth, one came to pray in the "martyrs' crypt" which, in the 19th century was adorned with mosaics. Alas, they are now quite dilapidated.

Mosaics in the Gallo-roman and civilisation museum, centre of the antique treasures of Lyons.

Lyon and all of its inhabitants including Guignol, Gnafron and their entire family, know the famous Gourguillon slope.

For many centuries, it was claimed that this name was due to the gurgling produced by the blood of martyrs which, during the persecutions of 177 and 202, had flowed down the slope of the hill as far as the Saône! This was still believed in the last century: the Fourvière mosaic which illustrates Saint Pothin's arrival in Lugdunum puts the amphitheater next to the Forum on which the Bossan basilica was built.

One had to wait until formal identification of the place where Blandine, Pontique and their brothers perished as the Croix-Rousse, so that finally the word Gourguillon (a gurgling sound) made one think of the sound of water flowing down the hill in stormy weather!

A Roman masterpiece : Saint-Martin d'Ainay.

For many centuries, one "searched" the "the martyrs' shaft" in the crypt of Saint-Irenaeus for the holy ground that, it was believed, was mixed with the ashes of the persecuted people of the 2nd and 3rd

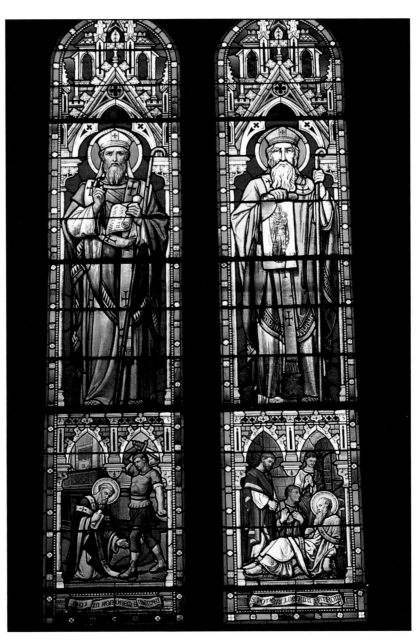

*Saint Pothin & Saint Irénée
immortalised in stained glass by Bégule
in the church of Saint-Nizier.*

centuries. Although very near this church there was an immense Roman and then Palaeo-Christian necropolis, the excavations carried out in this famous shaft have, alas, put an end to these pious traditions.

When, before the last war, a few young students and myself played at being archaeologists in the Fourvière excavations, we discovered a few human bones. While waiting for them to be dated, we entrusted them to the Sisters of a nearby convent.

- "Good Lord!" one of them exclaimed, amazed, "the bones of the martyrs of Lyon!"

A week later, two femurs, one tibia, three ribs, and one jaw were discovered to have been piously placed under the chapel's altarpiece.

A few months later, the excavations proved that this was not the martyrs' amphitheater, but the grand theater that we admire so much today. As to our discovery, it proved totally worthless!

The good Sisters remained unconvinced, and they continued to treasure bones which were more or less from the Middle Ages, as venerable holy relics.

But after all, why not respect, or even admire such convictions? They give proof of an inner faith: the Pope himself pointed this out.

In Lyon in the 2nd century and the years which followed during the High Middle Ages, there were numerous blood-baths of innocent people. History and most of its diligent readers know that others will follow: we will see examples of this further along in this book.

For the time being, let us leave the blood-red of the persecutions. The Romans adorned the city, and even today, certain remnants of the past captivate the unsuspecting visitor. In the nearby township of Saint-Foy-les-Lyon, in the place called Beaunand, the arches of an aqueduct cross the road and the Yzeron river. Its massive pillars date from Hadrian (the 2nd), and seem to rise up from a green prairie resplendent with flowers. And the fifteen hundred meters of Chaponost which strides across wheat fields, a prairie of numerous grasses, flowering with buttercups, are set out against the backdrop of a nursery of young conifers: in this place, the mind easily summons up the Roman countryside: only the sienna ochre of the earth, the dry grass and the raw-boned sheep of Latium are missing.

Immediately upon the death of Septimus Severus, in the 2nd century of our era, Lugdunum's decadence began.

The invasions, with Gaul forever being divided up between petty kings with their ephemeral power, the quarrels of the palace led to total anarchy, massacres and the "hideous famine". A few enlightened individuals nonetheless stood out above the darkness of these centuries of misery. The fair-haired

Burgundian Clothilde had her husband Clovis baptized. Bishop Nizier, the uncle of Grégoire de Tours, died in an aurora of holiness. At the foot of the Fourvière hill, Childebert and his wife Ultrogoth founded the Saunerie hospital, our first Hôtel-Dieu (6th century); the great bishop Leidrade, sent on a mission by Charlemagne, rebuilt the churches which had been devastated during invasions, and founded new ones; he also increased the number of schools whose purpose was to train clerics.

When the year 1 000 arrived, as everywhere in the West, Lyon, according to the famous statement of the monk Raoul Graber, "... shook itself, shed itself of its old tawdry finery and dressed up in a white mantle of the church!"

Let us imagine the Ainay Abbey, all new, and the cream-coloured stone of its blocks of limestone, the antique marbles recovered from the Roman monuments and which were used to build the apse of Saint-Jean, Saint-Paul and many churches destroyed by time, or by man...

However, little by little, the kings of France, following the lead of the Church and willing to share their power with the towns, after ever so many wars, unified our lovely country.

After a final martyr of whom François Villon sang with such rhapsody, that of

"Jeanne, la bonne Lorraine

qu'Englais brûlèrent à Rouen..." (Ballade des dames du temps jadis),

the sovereigns of our country, forgetting the ocean mists, turned their sights on the sunshine of Italy.

(1) As an impassioned archaeologist of rare learning, he spent his life excavating the ground of the city "in order" he said, "to bring Lugdunum and the ancient times of the Gauls' capital back to life". This was the son of the equally famous printer Marius Audin.

Previous page : a stained-glass window, with a very warm dominant blue colour.

34

The Golden Century of Lyon:
The Renaissance

III - The Golden Century of Lyon: The Renaissance

The "Tour rose", hôtel du Crible, sa remeniscent of Venice.

Since World War II, Lyon has understood that tourism was becoming one of the main "industries" of modern times. The city and its municipal officials, its artists and architects, its historians and writers, the curators of numerous museums have devoted themselves to one single mission: enticing art-loving tourists into the capital of the Gauls.

Lyon is gradually reaching this goal. To understand this, one has only to walk along our quays, our avenues, our old districts.

"The external walls of your buildings have as much make-up on as your fashionable ladies" I was told one day by an Austrian with a drawling voice due his stopovers in several famous cafés along the Saône. "And this house, all in red? It makes one think of a face of a Lyon denizen, which had taken on the colour of Beaujolais..."

The Virgin still protects the door to the temple which was to become the Celestins Convent in the XVIth century.

That very evening, my Austrian friend from Vienna told me, with some difficulties in French, of the marvels of the Saint-Stéphan cathedral, the Ring, the Belvédère and Schönbrunn, which, shamelessly, interfered with the Epicurean pleasures of Prater or the Heürigen of Grinzing.

We were sitting in the Bondy brasserie before a royal Gargantuan sauerkraut and a nice, foamy "sérieux" (king-size beer).

He spoke again of the colours of the city: they seemed to disturb his appetite and put a stop to the beginnings of a comfortable digestion. In the middle of the night, I led him back to the Louvre Hotel, opposite the Saône, which sparkled with the glittering of its precious stones; I told him to get a good night's sleep and put off a new stroll about Lyon until tomorrow.

The silk-workers know how to weave golden thread. (Maison des canuts)

Ten hours later, we met again near the Feuillée bridge.

- "Well then" said my Viennese acquaintance, "what kind of idea was that to colour your buildings this way?"

Personally, I thought that the Austrian testardise, after a proper digestion, was easily comparable to that of a Prussian jackass!

We went along the quays of the Saône, the Presqu'île, and even the Perrache district and its blockhouse... Then, we came back along left bank of the Rhône.

- "For a long time", I told him, "the city assumed a very ashen colour. Even now, some of the factory districts still have 'anemic, or even peeling facades: they are less and less numerous. The fine arts, the city and the department are doing their best to make this last shameful tawdry finery disappear!"

My friend was an educated man: I was able remind him of the most glorious period in the history of Lyon that he knew only very scantily.

Purple and gold brocades at the Maison des canuts.

The Basoche palace where attorneys meet.

- Charles VIII, Louis XII, François I and Henry II all dreamed of enlarging their kingdom to extend beyond the Alps and the Po plain. The political marriages of the 16th century, the treaties and alliances gave them the rights that they were to take advantage of.

Thus, the kings often came to Lyon, since if their dream had come true, the capital of their kingdom would have been placed judiciously in the center of their state, between the Rhône and Saône.

Chroniclers speak of the visits of these sovereigns to the city and their ostentatious stays.

For them, this involved hiring mercenaries, providing them with weapons, pay, food and lodging, and so forth.

As for our ancestors, forced to give in to the requirements of power, they tried to soften up the monarch through opulent receptions, and the wealthier ones even lent large amounts of money to their king, in return for substantial advantages.

In the "hôtel de la Couronne" (Crown Hotel) (town house dating back to the XVIth century), the Printing and Banking museum.

- "They were already capitalists" interrupted my Viennese friend, Otto.

- "That's true!", I conceded, "But the term "capitalist" did not have the "negative connotation" that it now has! During the Renaissance, the bourgeois were very rich, and long before Moliere, they sought the roles that their success could provide them with and which would ennoble them.

Louis XI had bestowed four annual fairs upon the city. French or foreign tradesmen came in great numbers. Since they were exempt from taxes, their businesses prospered. In Lyon, the Lombards, the Florentines, the Genoese and the Lucchese comprised what was called "the nations".

They built themselves luxurious hotels. Remember, Otto, the Laurencins, the Leviste hotels, all roughcast in beige and white, pink or cream-colours like Florentine houses; the Gadagnes hotel where the feasts were acclaimed; the Bullioud or Paterin hotel...

Thanks to these "bourgeois nobles", the city was governed and royal receptions were organized.

In a remarkable work entitled "When the Court of France Lived in Lyon" (Fayard, 1980), Louis Bourgeois includes a few lines about the splendors that Lyon lavished upon itself:

"In front of the Counselors, clothed in damask and crimson doublets, came German merchants clothed in gray woolen fabric, the Lucchese, in black damask, the Florentines, in velvet robes...

The streets were covered with cloth in the three colours of France, namely, white, yellow and red, which are the colours of the king..."

We would add that the loveliest women of Lyon were dressed in silk that Turquet and Nabriz were already producing all around the cathedral; they intermingled with all these personages, including the hallberdiers clothed in red, the musicians and the standard-bearers.

In the previous century, a new invention had taken the world by storm: the printing press. Rabelais had said of it: "Printing which is both elegant and correct... was invented in my time through divine inspiration..."

One hundred years later in Lyon, those who knew how to regroup the moveable letters which had been invented by Gutenberg in the middle of

Previous page :
Animation in historical quarters of
the town is forever on the rise

Le Gourguillon, "the fast road" up on the hill.

«The sky above the rooftops is so blue, so calm...» according to Verlaine.

the 15th century were very numerous. Far from Paris and the awful Sorbonne, the printers enjoyed precious freedom. People such as Alde Manuce, Guillaume Nourry (Rabelais' publisher), Sébastien Gryphe (who was to publish Etienne Dolet and Clément Marot), Barthélemy Buyer, Guillaume Rouville, Jean de Tourne (printer to Louise Labbé and Pernette du Guillet) were humanists. In addition to their mother tongue, they spoke, as Rabelais advised: "Greek, Latin, Hebrew, Chaldean, Arabic..." As ardent students of antiquity, they wanted to live according to the principles of Aristotle or Plato and revive Greco-Roman art in order to banish the art of the Middle Ages, that art which was as barbarian as that of the Goths and the ramblings of the sorbanâgres!

In 1500, the city already had fifty-three print shops; fifty years later, they were to number more than four hundred!

In the Printing and Bank Museum, organized by Maurice Audin, brother of the archaeologist, and thanks to the patronage of the Crédit Lyonnais bank,

44

we can admire their work, the tiny characters that they aligned so meticulously, their woodcuts and their illuminated illustrations, their book-bindings made of animal hide with titles in fine gold.

- "This museum", acknowledged Otto, "is quite famous on the other side of the Rhine, but the Mayence museum has the first Bible printed in the 16th century by Gutenberg!"

- "Yes, of course", I replied, "but ours, which by no seeks the ridiculous title of 'world-champion', can show its visitors the very first book printed in French and the first one to be illustrated with woodcuts, with an extraordinary realism. All these incussables are now known throughout the world. A very curious thing indeed: books with colours from the 16th century use only the colours of Lyon, that is, blue, red and yellow, and only very rarely green.

"Yes indeed," admitted Otto, "I must find time to explore this museum."

- "In addition", I added, "our humanist printers, as I told you, entertained writers who were just passing through our city, following the kings, their ministers and their generals. It is in their press that the Lyon literati of the Renaissance encountered one another. Louise Labbé, the lovely rope-dealer, who - even at that time - claimed equal rights for women, who loved with ardor and sang so well of passion in her admirable sonnets."

In the museum that we are speaking of, you will be able to see and admire the original editions of Maurice Scève and his young friend Pernette du Guillet, both poets.

Finally, among so many chefs-d'oeuvre, there is an extremely rare copy of the "placard contre la Messe" on display in a window; in 1534, it was placarded in the streets of Paris right up to the door of the cabinet of François I. Subsequent to this scandal, the persecution of the Huguenots began.

All these printers and humanists helped depict the Lyon Renaissance in gold!...

- "However", added my Viennese friend, "at that time, you had revolts of starving people, the persecution of the Huguenots, and papists were massacred - isn't that so?"

- "That's true," I had to admit, "but the revolt that you refer to, the "Grande rebeine", was the result of a disastrous harvest and the public disorders only lasted 10 days. If I may be so bold as to make a comment which, at first sight, appears contradictory, it had a rather happy ending! Our rich bourgeois of the period, these "privileged" persons, became aware of their duty! At the instigation of one of them, Jean du Peyrat, they brought together what was later to be called, "the body politic of misery". They decided to donate - freely and through a sense of devotion - a part of their income to help the poor. This very first example of charity, the " Aumône générale" lasted until the Revolution and was the predecessor of our present-day poorhouses.

- "That is absolutely astounding!" exclaimed Otto.

We had got back to the Saône. The sun had slipped behind the Fourvière basilica. The beams of light gave a pale reddish tint to the water.

- "My dear friend, we have spoken about the golden period of the Lyon Renaissance. However, other moments were frightfully blood-ridden. Right then, in the 16th century, there was a bridge which supported houses several stories high, inhabited by the members of the Reformed Churches. One week after the horrible Saint-Barthélemy massacre in Paris, the people turned against the Huguenots and massacred them. More than one hundred people had their throats slit, or were thrown from windows, leaving the river stained the river with blood. Tolerance was unknownat that time. When the Baron des Adrets seized the city, he quickly massacred the papists, violated the burial places, mutilated sculptures in the cathedral and numerous churches. But the very Catholic Blaise de Monluc, one of whose forts - since turned into a prison, it must be said! - bears the name, bragged about the number of Protestants he had hanged from trees in the cities and villages through which his troops had marched.

Otto the Viennese replied: "The land of Eden where the sky is cloudless, where young girls sing all throughout the day whilst dancing among the flowers, where women laugh and love endlessly... this exists only in the minds of poets!"

Next page :
the famous Philippe de l'Orme gallery.

Tant que mes yeux pourront larmes épandre
A l'heur passé avec toi regretter
Et qu'aux sanglots et soupir résister
Pourra ma voix et un peu faire entendre :

Tant que ma main pourra les cordes tendre
Du mignart lut pour tes graces chanter :
Tant que l'esprit se voudra contenter
De ne vouloir rien fors que toi comprendre :

Je ne souhaite encore point mourir.
Mais quand mes yeux je sentiray tarir
Ma voix cassée et ma main impuissante,

Et mon esprit en ce mortel séjour
Ne pouvant plus montrer signe d'amante :
Prirey la mort noircir mon plus beau jour.
Louise Labbé (Sonnet XIV)

The bloody period of the religious wars

D'où viens-tu Madelon ?
Elle vient, répond Jarrot,
D'estriper du huguenot
L'on me dit que ceux de Lyon
Vont tous en Avignon
Par le Rhône, sans bateau !
29th August 1572

My friend Otto returned to the city of music. He is still there, today, in the Place Gutenbert; if you manage to find his nameplate, you will see that since he stopped teaching at the university, he calls himself "Reiseführer". This German word has an unpleasant ring to it in French! But it merely means: "Tourist Guide"!

From the Royal Blue to the Blood-Red of «sans-culottes» (French Revolutionary republicans)

IV - From the Royal Blue to the Blood-Red of the "sans-culottes"
(French Revolutionary-Republicans)

The horses by Bartholdi, in the bronze-coloured lighting of the hôtel de ville, add to the greater glory of Hardoin-Mansart.

It was July, one of those stifling months that we often encounter in Lyon.

Her name was Lucia. On holiday in Lyon, she had come to the Carlton hotel with Paolo. Luigi, her husband, had created a high-fashion workshop in Milan. He had not been able to come with her.

Her shining eyes, her gleaming lips and dimples laughed endlessly. Each and every one of her phrases was like a song!

- "I am going to entrust you with an Italian lady who is as lovely as one of Raphael's virgins," my friend Simon had said. "What's more, she is delightful, but she wants to know everything about tne city. She has already visited the Roman theaters of the Fourvière and the Croix-Rousse amphitheater, including Ainay and the cathedral; now she wants to see the center, visit the museum... She's killing me! Please, take over for a While!"

I recalled this request and the meeting which followed it when I saw her appear under one of the cloister's arcades. "I'll be back, tomorrow morning! I shall spend the morning and afternoon in your museum! There are so many chefs-d'oeuvre to admire!"

We reached the Place des Terreaux. The bell in the belfry had just sounded four o'clock. The sun turned the granite in the square leaden, silver-plated the water in the Bartholdi fountain and the small modern sprays created by Buren! The facade of the Town Hallseemed to have been crackled under the harsh light of summer.

Lucia and I sat down at the terrace of a café and ordered cold drinks.

- "What a lovely square!" said my friend.

- "It only dates back to the 17th century. Before that, there was an enormous empty lot here, around which ran the city ditch: a real sewer! local archers, and later the musketeers, trained here. The pork mar-

Frontings on Bellecour square rebuilt by Bonaparte after their destruction during the Revolution.

51

The silent cloisters where the ghost of Rabelais roams.

ket was ideally located near this ditch as one could get rid of the bloody, stinking innards. Additionally, in some cases, one beheaded brigands, false salniers, or unrepentant villains.

On September 12th 1642 in this place, one beheaded Cinq Mars and de Thou who had betrayed France and hated Richelieu. From the scaffold, the two convicted men waved to the crowd, kept back by one hundred of the consulate's archers; they blew kisses to the ladies, showing extraordinary bravery!

- "It's too bad you didn't have a Carraletto or a Guardi to immortalize this horrible scene!" broke in Lucia.

- "Yes, even more so in that accounts from this period report that the two tortured prisoners wore 'brown clothes on Dutch woolen fabric, covered with gold lace... green silk stockings and a scarlet coat...!

It was then that the consulate decided to purchase a vast "Town House", suitable for a large city. Simon Maupin built the first real Palais Municipal (Town Hall). It took him nearly sixteen years. Hardly

In the night, the facade of the hôtel-Dieu, seen from the bridge over the Rhône. The great dome was bombed during the Revolution and burned during Liberation.

was it finished when it was ravaged by fire. That was when Hardouin-Mansart stepped in.

- "The one responsible for Versailles? the Place Vendôme? the Invalides?" my companion exclaimed.

- "Precisely! He is responsible for the Town Hall; you can admire its noble facade, its pavilions and its roofs covered with slate; the balustrades of its terraces and its belfry tower crowned with a sort of tiara with a golden crest. While it was being built, an enormous building was completed at the southern angle of the external wall. Formerly, this had been an unassuming convent. In the 17th century, a young abbess, Anne de Chaulnes, daughter of a Marshal of France and niece of the Duke of Luynes, friend of Louis XIII, decided to rebuild this abbey of the canonesses of Saint-Pierre for whom she was responsible. Royer de la Valfenière, an architect from Avignon who loved Italy, was in charge of the construction. He built this ascetic facade two hundred meters long, evenly separated by pilasters with Corinthian capitals and crowned with a balustrade overlooked by a small, italien-style belvedere.

Before undertaking the construction of this austere but elegant facade, Madame de Chaulnes had obtained a promise from the Consulate to build a public square in front of the monastery. The city leveled the compost piles and filled in the ditches. It is thus to this very noble abbess that we owe this square in the very center of the city.

- "But why these shops?" asked Lucia. "They spoil this facade."

- "They already existed in the 17th century. The Saint-Pierre canonesses sold the wine from their vineyards there. For these ladies "lived nobly". Each of them had a servant who was housed in a corner of their vast cell: she fulfilled the role allotted to Saint Martha in the Gospel! Also, the decoration of the refectory and the chapel had cost a great deal of money.

In the 17th century, thanks to the Council of Trent and the Edict of Nantes, the growth of Protestantism had been halted. Lyon was a city of convents: the names of our squares and our streets bear witness to this: rues des Augustins, des Carmélites, des Feuillants... Places des Célestins, des Cordeliers, des Jacobins (Dominicans), among others. As early as the beginning of this century, the Jesuit Martelange rebuilt the Collège de la Trinité donated by Henry IV to the Fathers of the Society of Jesus; it has since become our Ampère lycée!

We reached the "Moulin joli" at the corner of the square. And there, a little away from the overcrowded bar, she sat down and ordered: "A halfbottle of champagne! Fresco, prego!"

"I have told you about the pleasant periods in Lyon, but there were also bloodthirsty periods; during the Revolution, the city lived through the 'colors' of assassinations, massacres, the guillotine!"

The French Revolution was initially rather well-received by our fellow citizens of the 18th century. They welcomed the idea of equality before the Law; they expected lower taxes, work for everyone, more abundant food. Alas, this was a far cry from reality!

- "When a project which one holds dear," broke in Lucia, "stems from dreams, it is transformed into illusions!"

- "You are talking like a philosopher!" I replied. "I wasn't really expecting this of you!"

Lucia burst into laughter; this silvery laughter wich so enchanted me. Nonetheless, I continued my story.

- "Most citizens of Lyon were Catholic and did not regret the passing of the obsolute monarchy; they even praised the Constitution, but only until the Pope denounced it; then came the flight of the king and his arrest; the Republic was proclaimed and more or less accepted between the Rhone and Saône; on the other hand, when, in Paris, the extremists declared war, executed their more moderate

The new opera of Jean Nouvel.

opponents and guillotined the king, the people of Lyon rose up in rebellion, Fanatics such as Chalier and his friends were sent to the scaffold.

Lyon then rose up against Paris: the city had to be taken by force. It was besieged by thirty thousand men and a sizable artillery force. It defended itself heroically, but, after seventy days, capitulated.

Then the came the reign of Terror. A decree was issued, proclaiming the imminent destruction of all the wealthy residences in the city. This is the famous Decree of October 13th 1793.

The terrible decree of the 21st day of the 1st month of Year II (Extracts) (October 12th 1793)

Art. 2 - The city of Lyon shall be destroyed; everything which was inhabited by the wealthy shall be demolished; there shall remain only the poorhouse, the residences of patriots who have gone astray or who were been banished, buildings used specially for industry and monuments dedicated to humanity and to civic instruction.

Art. 4 - The name of Lyon shall be erased from the list of cities in the Republic; the union of 'preserved houses' shall henceforth bear the name of the Emancipated City.

Art. 5 - On the ruins of Lyon, there shall be built a column which shall remind posterity of the crimes and punishment of the royalists of this city, with the following inscription :

"Lyon fought against Freedom ; Lyon is no more."

The Revolutionary Tribunal sat in this lovely Town Hall. Its cellars overflowed with arrested suspects. The guillotine, set up on the Place des Terreaux, was active from daybreak to sunset. Hatchets or sabers were used to massacre the unfortunate innocent victims on the stairway of the Town Hall. An engraving of the period shows a "sans-culotte" proffering the head of an aristocrat to a woman of the people, with dogs lapping up the "blue blood" on the wooden paving stones of the square...

- "How awful!" exclaimed Lucia. Her eyes glistened ; she was on the verge of crying. She drank half her glass and seemed to regain her composure in the golden bubbles of the champagne. "In all countries," she added, "in all cities, in spite of the days of glory, the blood-stained days leave atrocious memories!"

- "Thus, our Town Hall was used as a prison and special tribunal. More than two thousand "self-style

The "Loge du Change", an example of the talent of Soufflot.

aristocrats" were executed on this square that we crossed a few moments ago. Even today, I know Lyon citizens who are proud of their nobiliary particle and who refuse to cross a certain corner of the square where the guillotine lopped off heads and executed their ancestors!" (In the south-east part, at the opening of the Constantine and Paul Chenavard streets).

Paolo rose on his four curly paws : he was bored! His mistress and I got up and left the Moulin Joli.

- "I should like to return to the Carlton along the Rhone quay," said Lucia.

Crossing the Place Louis Pradel, she stared at the facades, the Ipousteguy fountain, the statue of Louis Labbé, the monument to "the lyonnaiseries", the stream, the flower beds...

- "But what a strange way to decorate the roof your opera!", she cried. "Did you have a leftover

Satolas airport hangar which had to be reused ? Whithout this ugly scrap iron, the facade must have been quite lovely !"

- "One tried to enlarge the "Grand Théâtre", so dear to the people of Lyon, in order to equip the rehearsal rooms for singers from choruses, ballet troupes, and so forth. The black and red interior and its immense offwhite stage curtain have more character !"

- "Nonetheless, seen from Fourvière, yesterday, this hangar and your Part-Dieu tower, that horrible rocket which is just too massive to take off, make the surroundings so ugly !"

I did not wish to dispute this reproach ; but I hate to criticize the city where I was born, I remained silent ; I was fond of it ! I would prefer that it be esteemed without the slightest reservation !

We crossed the Jean Moulin quay, Lucia admired the mighty river and its force, although its level was nonetheless rather low, as is the case every summer.

"This remarkable river," I told her, "reminds me of some lines from the poet Maurice Sève who (see the previous chapter) wrote during the Renaissance :

"Tu cours superbe, à Rhone fleurissant

En sable d'or et argentines eaux,

Ceint de cités et bordé de châteaux..."

- "In front of your Palais du Commerce I saw a bas-relief representing a naked man, very muscular, swimming ardently and holding tight against his body a woman who seemed to be unconscious. At the reception desk at the Carlton, I was told that this was the river and its Lyon tributary.

- "In fact, Lucia, the sculptor Vermare wanted to symbolize the Saône engulfed by the triumphal Rhone which it carried along to the sea. Some people find the brutality of this sculpture rather macho !"

The sun had begun its evening promenade : the lengthening shadows turned pink. When we reached the hospital, the Rhone was dappled with gold. My companion wondered aloud about the long facade of the great slate-gray dome framed between the leaves of plane trees along the Jules Courmont quay.

- "Who are these majestic personages between the columns ?"

- "Those are two statues from the last century -

The Ainay Vaults where the battling people of Lyons came to pick up supplies during the siege in 1793.

King Childebert and his wife who answers to the "delightful" first name of Ultrogothe. In the 6th century, they founded the first hospital for the poor. But this facade, which is over three hundred meters long, is the work of the architect Germain Soufflot. He worked in Lyon in the 18th century before being summoned to Paris by Louis XV. He is also responsible for the Loge des Changeurs at the foot of the Fourvière hill and several magnificent mansions built for the rich bourgeoisie of his time.

To return to the Hôtel-Dieu, you should go through its courtyards and visit its excellent museum. Perhaps you will find a little of your own country there ! In fact, the central part was built using the drawings of Ospedale Maggiore from Milan, who was admired by a Lombard who had emigrated between the Rhone and Saône, César Laure.

We reached Bellecour. Lucia admired the bronze statue of King Louis XIV.

- "He sits astride his horse in front of a noble facade and the greenery on the hill which, in the background, is like a pedestal for your basilica !

Night was beginning to fall. The lights shone brightly in the windows of the houses. Suddenly, Notre-Dame de Fourvière and then the metal tower were lit up.

- "The colors of Lyon : what a wonder !" said my lovely Italian. "Your squares are clothed in pink sand, your external walls change from creamy white to scarlet red, depending on the taste of the owners ; in this city, one finds the entire range of greens, starting with the bronze on the statues up through the light-green leaves of the lime trees or plane trees ; the mounds and flower beds are like fantastic mosaics and, when evening comes, and then the night, the lighting forms shadows and causes the various hues to blaze up.

In the gardens of Saint-Peter's palace,
which now houses the Fine Arts Museum.

The Black Flag of
the Flat Bellies

V - The Black Flag of the Flat Bellies

Pastel-coloured façades in the rue des Fantasques.

The first two weeks of October had just ended. It was nearly five o'clock: Sunday had been quite mild. With friends from Burgundy, we went through the center of the Croix-Rousse district in a haphazard way, ambling along like people out for a stroll.

We had entered the St-Denis church. Then, from there, we went to number 83 in the Grande Rue, this quaint garden dedicated by an Andelusian mason to Rosa Mir, his mother.

Ivy and Virginia creepers embraced the columns of the pergolas that the mauve-colored wisteria had invaded. At the foot of the walls with shell and fossil insets, nasturtiums, begonias and pansies bedecked the ground with the colors of marble from Alhambra, or opulent carpets from the East.

- "How naive," said Blandine, a photographer from Dijon.

Jacquard who totally transformed the weaving loom

- "Not at all", replied Augustin, her husband, who as a doctor in medicine, zealously explored the mysteries of psychoanalysis. This work is due to an uncontrollable and thus spontaneous gushing of an impulse, due to the absent love of absent or perhaps even dead mother! This urge obviously emanates from the surrealistic threshold of her sensorial ego!

Alexander and Sandrine, both pharmacists in Beaune, Jean-Louis and Pierrette remained silent, but their faces showed that they were dying to laugh. I had then defused the mockery by saying: "My word, in such priceless terms are truths uttered!"

Quite relaxed, we had entered the house of the Canutes and the third couple in our group, Augustin and Blandine, who sold flowers in Montbard, admired - even more than our other friends - the lavish lampas, moiré damask, iridescent velvets...

We then reached the boulevard where fashion held forth. The crowd pressed on...

The crowd pressed on, laughed, hummed the old songs gushing forth from the loud speakers; the wooden horses went round and round in magic stampedes and the children were delighted; the little train made its short journey slowly and blew its whistle each time it passed in front of the "miniature train station"; the owner of the raffle stand promised prizes to all the players; the "hair-raising" train frightened only the "under five's" or the "teens" who wanted to play at being afraid; there were dodgems involved in horrible mad scrambles or harmless pileups, which did not even phase the young girls.

Sugary fragrances came from the "Alps candy shop" where a pretty mulatto stretched multicolored strips of candy which she cut with a pair of scissors.

- "Real boiled sweets from Lyon!" she exclaimed.

- "Why do you say they are from Lyon?" asked a visitor, with the Tartarin accent.

- "The blue, white and red!" answered the clever confectioner laughing out loud!

Further on, merguez sausages sizzled in the blue smoke rising over the incandescent charcoal of a brazier. Near the statue of Jacquard, we bought finely-roasted chestnuts. Their hulls crackled like parchment.

- "In Lyon", I told the friends who were with me, "'châtaignes' (a 'sweet' chestnut) are called 'marrons' (another kind of chestnut used for cooking) and the white wine which goes with them is called 'mâconnais'!"

We thus acquiesced to the noble tradition on the terrace of the "Café des Ecoles".

That was when Augustin and Blandine, who

Live and work or die fighting.
Monument to the silk-weavers, Croix-Rousse.

cour des Voraces

were worn out, took leave of absence via an exhausting route on the plateau between the roundabouts, and Jean-Louis and Pierrette, one complaining of varicose veins and the other of her new shoes, decided to return to the center by underground.

The two survivors, Alexander and Sandrine his wife, did not sell Mâconnais but "patent medicines" at their shop just steps away from the famous Hôtel-Dieu. Together we stopped off at the "Gros Caillou".

- "I once knew," I expounded, "one of Mayor Herriot's deputies who, at the age of 6, actually saw this famous monument being put up. He told me that in 1890, a passage was dug, intended for a new funicular railway, now partly used by the underground line. The pickaxes ran up against a stone which put up a stiff resistance. Sparks flew: the road-workers did not insist. It was an erratic block abandoned by glaciers at a time when dinosaurs meandered over the

Rosa Mir garden, by the humble mason Avidalou.
Previous page : coming down the "Grand'Côte" (big hill).

plateau which, several thousand years later, was baptized the Croix-Rousse... Fifteen cattle from the Limousin, hitched up in threes, rolled this weight up to the boulevard... the block was placed on a plinth... Since then, the Giant Pebble has been perched on its throne... and is quite comfortable there, thank you. On May 1st every year from 1895 to 1905, it was painted red in honor of the festival which, at that time, was called "revolutionary"; the rain took care of restoring its natural color, and for some time, the Giant Pebble cried tears of blood!"!

Alexander was nearly two meters tall; this is why we baptized him "Alexander-the-Great Potard". •

- "What a priceless souvenir!" he exclaimed. "Your witness of times past must have been very old!"

- "No, not so" I pointed out. "This octogenarian wore a black jacket whose buttonhole was decorated with a red ribbon won in the war of 1914-1918, a pair of striped trousers, a loosely-knotted bow-tie with white spots at the neck. He was forever smiling, happy with his life in the service of the Plateau. The index and middle fingers of his right hand were always yellow, since he smoked non-stop." "Smoked meat", he affirmed, "is preserved better than other kinds!" He died in his sleep some ten years later!"

- "Nonetheless, said Sandrine, "nicotine is a poison!"

- "He gave me another version of the origin of the Giant Pebble. A Lyon citizen "des autres fois" (an old expression among us. Translation: a Lyon citizen of times gone by) by the name of Jean Tourmente was so mean throughout his life that, when he appeared before the Great Judge, the latter sentenced him to push his horrific soul, all puffed up with his sins, across the city. The punishment came to an end just at the end of the boulevard, and there, the soul of the reprehensible sinner was turned to stone! Jean Tourmente was a "bumbailiff" on the rue Mercière, which in the Canute language means bailiff!"!

Weavers house with its high profile required for the Jacquard loom.

Behind the Giant Pebble, we admired the countryside. The autumn mists rose over the Rhone, gliding between the plane trees on the quays, threading their way among the streets in the Brotteaux district. The roofs turned pink and the facades took on pastel colors. The foliage of the Tête d'Or mixed the gold and red with the most variegated shades of green. A few thin plumes of smoke coiled up in the sky. The sun had gone to bed in the west, and dimmed its lamp. On the horizon, the Alps had disappeared. In spite of the hullabaloo of the village fête, we heard the clock strike six...

We quickly reached number 9 on the Place Colbert, the famous courtyard of the Voraces, recently restored.

"We were told about this in Beaume, " said Sandrine, "but we didn't know anything about it!"

"This is the most famous of Canute buildings," I pointed out. "You must admit, this facade is impressive, with a stairway open to the wind, skipping from one landing to another, up six stories. It is supported by solid monolithic pillars and separated by vast rectangular openings. There were four or five workshops on each floor. The looms, transformed by Jacquard, were quite naturally installed under French-style ceilings located at just the right height."

"So" broke in Alexander-the-Great-Potard, "this means that there are nearly a hundred people occupying the building"?

"Yes, that's right, but these silk workers were not the most downtrodden. Through the openings along the stairway, the air could reach them in their workplaces and the windows of the rear facade, with a southern exposure, provided them with light. And then, what was very exceptional at that time, there was a place for "group" relaxation on each floor!"

I then spoke about the "canuserie". We were sitting quietly on a step on this famous stairway. Evening was approaching, casting mysterious shadows in the secret corners of the courtyard.

In the area where silk was being manufactured, one could see the manufacturers and the weavers, working alone or under the supervision of the workshop foremen.

But - and this seemed highly original! - the silk-manufacturers did not manufacture; they merely ordered their items, paid for them and sold them... at the best possible prices.

As for the weavers, they carried their work to the

manufacturers on their shoulders and were paid... in the traditional "thrifty" manner of Lyon!

When the craftsman admired his piece of silk, so delicate to the sense of touch, so heavy to carry, he marveled at the lavish drawings, the opulent colors, the changing reflections of the moiré fabric and he was proud of his work, but he felt - already! - that his know-how was poorly recompensed, all the more so in that, in order to live even meagerly, he had to work fifteen to eighteen hours a day...

It has been said that in order to purchase 1 kilogram of bread and a few vegetables, one needed one franc per day. But the weaver, when he received an order, received between 50 centimes and 1 franc 50 centimes!

In November 1831, the cup which had been full for so long, overflowed! The Croix-Rousse Canutes, the most numerous at that time, left their commune (which was still independent of Lyon) and went down to the Prefecture at the "côte St-Sébastien" then situated at the present location of our Place des Jacobins. Faced with a crowd of shrieking weavers, and heeding the advice of the Prefect Bouvier-Dumolart, the manufacturers accepted a better price and even went so far as to sign deeds to this effect.

As soon as the demonstrators had returned to their workshops, they realized that the new price was not being enforced.

So there was another demonstration. But, at the Rue Vielle Monnaie (our present Rue Roger Leynaud) and at the corner of the côte St-Sébastien, the National Guard and the army fired on them.

People were killed. Others were marched through the streets. The workers then pillaged the arms factories, the military barracks, the powder magazine and swore to avenge their martyrs...

They united around the black flag of the downtrodden and on which they painted the formula which was soon to become an immortal slogan: "Live by one's work, or die fighting".

We left the Voraces building via its exit on the Rue Imbert Colomès, and reached the grounds of the former Villemanzy military hospital.

Night was now falling over the city. On the external walls, the windows lit up one by one, and the plane trees, illuminated by the spotlights, assumed their golden finery for the night.

"But why," asked Alexander-the-Great-

The silk-weavers environment where the clickety-clack of the loom resounded for 15 hours every day.

Schoolboy, "has this house and its courtyard been called the house of the gluttons?"

- "Oh," I answered, "this is a story which goes well back beyond the terrible events that we have just spoken of. In 1840, coachmen, carriers, porters or other donkey-boys gathered to quench their bottomless thirst chez Mère Marshal, a Croix-Rousse keeper of a restaurant for the poor, or in various other public-houses on the plateau. But some of these crafty tradesmen decided to sell the wine by the liter and no longer by the jar. This cost the thirsty workers more than they had been used to paying. In addition, the Lyon jar did not have a clear-cut capacity... Thus, the customers of Mère Marshal started a quarrel, banged their fists on the table, and shouted their anger. "Those men are real gluttons (voraces)" said their compatriots. And the name had been found! The gluttons, sure that they were within their rights, gathered together in groups to slake their thirst; but little by little, their meetings became political. Louis Philippe's bobbies watched them very carefully, and in the building that we have just left, there was talk of the Republic; it was welcomed ecstatically in 1848.

If you don't mind, we will return to our rebellious Canutes. Next to the esplanade where we are now, they suffered a great many losses and the shooting which took place at the Bernardines convent (which preceded the Villemanzy military hospital) has remained sadly famous. In its present redeveloped state, the city now welcomes foreign intellectuals there, who come to work in our libraries or our laboratories. All the workers from the suburbs and all districts in the city gathered together at the Croix-Rousse. The barricades increased in number; the

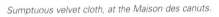

Sumptuous velvet cloth, at the Maison des canuts.

"Traboule" (narrow, covered
passage-way)
in the Croix-Rousse area

fighting was savage, but the insurgents finally won. The authorities and soldiers abandoned the Town Hall which was then occupied by the Canutes. There was no pillage since possible thieves were warned: they would be put to death.

- "How did all that end?" asked Sandrine.

- "The insurgents had no real leaders, and those at the head of the movement did not all have the same ideas about how to materialize their victory. Paris sent the Duke of Orleans to Lyon; he was the son of Louis-Philippe and Marshal Soult, heroes of the imperial wars. The army re-established order and the number of arrests increased. The Canutes were only victorious for... 9 days!"

In 1834, there was another revolt as a result of a trial in which silk workers stood accused. This new revolt was even more dreadful than the preceding one. General Aimard's 10 000 troupes massacred the poor. The Passage de l'Argue was cleaned out by gun fire. The Cordeliers church door was blown up in order to butcher those who had taken refuge within. And the bloodthirsty Prefect Gasparin was to declare to the government: "Our operations are finished; we have restored peace to the city!"

The "operations" had killed nearly 300 civilians or military personnel!

Although our great city has experienced its moments of glory, it has not always been spared blood-strewn streets!

We reached the Place Croix Paquet. There was a large sign on the 1st floor of a building indicating the headquarters of the "Association for the Right to Housing".

- Today, as in the past, the same problems remain: people out of work are helped for a few months, and then sent back to the street without any resources. Let us hope that employment picks up before new revolts break out like those of the 19th century!

Night had fallen on the Place des Terreaux. The granite paving-stones, polished by the water and its little luminous sprays, assumed the aspect of marble; the Bartholdi horses reared up in the blue foam and, on her splendid cart, "the river goddess" triumphed in the glory of the spotlights which bathed both the front of the Town Hall facade and the Palais des Arts.

- "Lyon is lovelier at night than by day!" exclaimed Sandrine.

VI - The "Gray-Green" Years

The Célestins theatre hidden behind the rhododendrons on the new square.

The film-maker Claude Berri made a film commemorating the glory of the Lyon Renaissance and one of its heroines, Lucie Aubrac. To accomplish this, it was necessary to bring a few parts of the occupied city back to life...

Red banderoles with the swastika hung on either side of the Town Hall. At the top of its belfry floated the flag of nazi Germany. The mechanized troops of the diabolic Führer marched through our avenues, the field-gray uniforms, and the short hobnailed boots marched through our streets. Sometimes there were even the doleful tubas, the

deafening guns of the heavy artillery, the Prussian fifes and Teutonic trumpets resounded in our public squares along with the military marches which were then triumphal!

This was in June 1940; once again Lyon had been occupied.

The first time - at least in the modern era - was by French partisans of the Parisian members of the National Convention (see Chapter 4). Then Napoleon, in spite of Champaubert, Montmirail and numerous other victories, was crushed; forty thousand Austrians occupied the city. The white flag of the Bourbons was raised over the Town Hall.

During the Hundred Days, the French red, white and blue flag reappeared, again replacing the flag

The Stone Watchman.

of the kings at the final fall of the Empire, until Charles X abandoned his throne to Louis-Philippe, the bourgeois king who demanded the return to the three colors.

After which, there were several "interludes" with the black flag of the poor, or even the red flag...

But as of the Second Empire, the real red, white and blue flag floated over the city, "once and for all" it was thought!

In 1914, war broke out. Like the Parisians, the Lyon citizens went off to battle with "a flower in the gun-barrel" for what one thought would be an immediately victorious outing. The butchery was to last four years!

The hospitals were soon overcrowded. The authorities organized temporary hospitals in the available buildings. In the factories, the women replaced the men who had been called to defend the country - Herriot, mayor of Lyon since 1905, convinced like his citizens of victory, recreated 1916 Exposition, although Verdun had once again been conquered. The city lamented the death of 10 600 young men.

They were mourned... Tony Garnier and Jean Larrivé built them a glorious cenotaph on an island in the Tête d'Or park. They were mourned... but, this time, it was the "war to end all wars" and there would never be any more!

Alas, then came the nazi plague, and twenty years later, one had to "start all over again"!

Hitler's armies invaded France; they surged into Lyon via the Croix-Rousse and the quays. The first occupation was to last from June 18th to July 7th. Marshal Pétain received full power by 569 votes to 80, and tried to reorganize the country. After the armistice, the city became the capital of a non-occupied zone.

As of September 1942, it put the gray-green uniforms back on along with the short boots, the armbands with the swastika, the skull-and-crossbones of the SS, subsequent to the Anglo-American liberation of North Africa...

Henceforth, resistance to the occupying forces began to get organized; Jean Moulin managed to unite all members of the resistance before being arrested in Caluire by the Gestapo and the sinister

Klaus Barbie; he was tortured and died without disclosing any information. The interrogations took place in the Ecole de Santé Militaire where there is now a museum so that the victims of national-socialism are not forgotten and, above all, so that never again will the "bloodthirsty hydra of fascism" return.

The nazis - helped alas by Frenchmen who betrayed the France of Freedom - pursued all those who refused to submit. Many of our compatriots, disheartened by political scandals in the period between the two World Wars, remained chary.

Near the Place des Terreaux, at N° 12 Rue Ste-Catherine, a marble plate commemorates one of the most monstrous days of the year 1943.

The Jewish community had organized here a mutual assistance center to help the less fortunate of its members. But the nazis, who had long ago decided to annihilate all Israelites for the simple reason-

The University, the students of which took an active part in Resistance.

79

that they practiced the religion of Moses, because many of them, due to their talent or their work, had become wealthy and that they had been able to keep certain traditions, dating back thousands of years, preciously intangible... On February 9th 1943, in this building early in the morning, the Germans, backed by members of the French militia, arrested eighty hapless men, women and innocent children. Almost all of them were to die during deportation!

Resistance was impossible. The crime had been well-organized, the surprise was total and the fascist weapons would have spat death without the slightest hesitation! Nonetheless, the struggle against the dictatorship was to become generalized in spite of torture and executions. The enemy troops were attacked. In the factories, the workers slowed down or even sabotaged production. Resistance networks such as Libération, Franc-tireur, Combat and others, attacked troop or merchandise transports destined for Germany, for the factories which worked for Hitler, the nazi agents and their French henchmen.

General de Gaulle's partisans increased in number. However, the call of June 18th 1940 had only resulted in sarcastic comments in Lyon, as in the rest of France: how could one war when the entire country had been invaded? Little by little, hope was born and courage revived the vanquished.

As early as 1942, there was a very auspicious demonstration in the center of the city and in front of the Town Hall. The Germans, thinking that there the entire French population was collaborating with them, had sent to Lyon the Berlin Philharmonic Orchestra and its orchestra leader, Clémens Kraus. Our compatriots swore to prevent this unbecoming propaganda concert from taking place. The police managed to break up the crowd of dissidents who shouted their hatred on the Place des Terreaux and just outside the Salle Rameau. The artists from across Rhine nonetheless managed to play Wagner for two hours. But four-fifths of their listeners were policemen or collaborators!

One week after this demonstration, and in this same room, Paul Paray directed the Witkowski Orchestra in a concert of exclusively French music. This unleashed a wave of enthusiasm beyond description. After five encores, this magnificent orchestra leader turned to his musicians, his baton raised like an avenging two-edged sword.

- *"The 'Marseillaise'"*, he shouted, "in B flat!".

Then, before these stalls, these boxes and its packed balconies, where eight days earlier, the trombones of Tannhaüser had resounded, the crowd of Lyon citizens assembled, supported by its orchestra and directed by Paray, started shouting all its hope and its hatred for the occupant by an extremely emotional rendering of the national anthem. As of that day, one began to feel that the dark days of Lyon under the German heel were numbered.

The prisoners of war had not been freed. The nazis deported nearly 8 000 young people to the other side of the Rhine. There they were treated like Spartan Helots, that is, starved and despised. They had to work - and "did as little as possible!" - under the allied bombs which were paving the way to victory. Still, their plight could not be compared with the fate of those condemned to die in the extermination camps.

At the Place Bellecour, the Café du Moulin à Vent was frequented by nazi troops and collaborators. The Resistance blew it up on July 27th 1944. There were only material damages. The next day, five members of the Resistance chosen by lot in the German jails were shot under the eyes of passers-by in front of the demolished café. Their names were: Chambonnet, Bernard, Pfeffer, Dru, Chirat. The youngest was just 21 years of age! Their bodies, drenched in blood, were to remain on the pavement for many hours without permission even being given to cover them with a sheet! Thanks to Cardinal Gerbier, they were subsequently taken to the morgue; this priest had threatened the German general in charge with putting put their bodies in his own car.

In addition to those who were shot, tortured and deported, Lyon also suffered horrible bombardments, resulting in more than 1 000 victims, with the destruction of some 450 buildings.

Lyon, the city of golden colors had - alas! - along with the gray-green of the occupants, experienced the tears of blood and the blood-red of the conflagrations in the very center of residences which had been lain to waste or left in ruin.

Finally the city was liberated, but only after extensive suffering and grief.

Claude Berri's film therefore reminds us that Lucie Aubrac, this outstanding heroine who led the clandestine struggle in defiance of all forms of danger! Her husband Raymond was one of Jean Moulin's right-hand men; Moulin was General de Gaulle's envoy, who, along with André Lassagne, was arrested in Caluire at the home of Doctor Dugoujon. Thanks to his wife and his friends in the Corps francs de la Résistance, Aubrac was twice snatched from the Gestapo at the last minute.

Even though this film gives a quite accurate picture of what these "gray-green years" were really like, people in Lyon who had experienced the occupation were relieved when the film was finished: the Place des Terreaux returned to normal, the flag with the swastika disappeared, the little fountains sprang to life again, the lorries, the jack boots, the steel helmets faded away... in the light of a city, which indeed has its problems, but which is free.

There are memories that one would prefer to see snuffed out by the mists of time, and erased forever!

Rue René Leynaud, named after a young journalist and Resistant shot by the Nazis in 1944.

Festive Lyon,
in the Colours of Happiness

VII - Festive Lyon,
in the Colours of Happiness

The writer Pierre Emile Legrand, who delighted his compatriots with his zany plays (like those of Guignol), and encouraged their optimism through his "psychological analyses" full of good common sense, thus defines the gones (brash kids) among us:

> «On dit que les «Yonnais» sont gens tristes et froids,
> Avares, méfiants et même un peu sournois,
> Qu'un intense brouillard des Brotteaux à Fourvière
> Assombrit leur cité comme leur caractère.
> C'est pas vrai, nom d'un rat, les gones de chez nous
> Sont ni des constipés, ni des cogne-mous !
> S'ils crânent un peu moins que nos «capitalistes»
> Et si des Marseillais souvent un peu fumistes,
> Ils n'ont ni la faconde ni l'air avantageux,
> C'est que, modestement, ils se trouvent heureux.
> Avoir de bons amis avec qui on lichotte,
> Ou bien, le soir venu, embrasser sa fenotte.
> Loin des caquenanauds curieux et médisants :
> Voilà notre bonheur bien simple et bien canant.»

Our city loves cheerfulness and subscribes to the declaration: "Laughter is specific to man!"

Perhaps one will find the humor a little too heavy-handed in Vaise, the Guillotière or the Croix-Rousse; somewhat narrow-minded in the Brotteaux or in Ainay; often sanctimonious, in Fourvière or in St-Jean... but these are assertions which are too systematic, stereotyped and ultimately, totally groundless...

84

In Lyon, one speaks French, but you don't say «la foire» you say «la vogue».

Saint-Georges carnaval.

Lyon has always known how to laugh and enjoy festivals.

We pointed this out earlier: in the past, the excursions of kings between the Rhône and Saône involved marvelous receptions with fairy-like floats carrying the loveliest of women, lavish costumes, fanfares, songs, cheers and flowers right down to the most impoverished houses. For major occasions, there were fountains of wine which provided drink to everyone who was thirsty, without having to spend a penny. Festivals have always been numerous between the Rhône and Saône. There ware balls and tournaments in the "Grenette", in the "Juiverie", or in the "Brotteaux". The fairs took place in a happy, care-free mood. The Tupiniers fair (celebrating ceramic jars) brought back to life in modern times near the cathedral, or, yet again, the St-Georges carnival, are proof of Lyon's gaiety.

During the festival, pennants, horsemen and horsewomen dressed in Renaissance garments crossed through the city; the banners of the various districts or guilds flap in the wind; only a few years ago,

Guignol : still stands for good humour. At the Cardelli Museum, rue Saint-Jean.

Mourguet the tooth-puller, inventor of Guignol, as depicted at the tiny Cardelli Museum, rue Saint-Jean.

an outstanding show on the Place Bellecour stirred memories of the splendor of yesteryear. On the national holiday on July 14th, the night sky is lit up with fireworks set off in Fourvière, drawing crowds of people to the Saône quay.

Even more than these lay festivals, the religious festivals, rich in colour, continue to be respected traditions between the Plateau and the Hill.

As early as the Middle Ages, the most famous festival was that of the Merveilles. This was held on June 2nd for the Festival of St-Pothin, the first Bishop of Lugdunum. On the Saône, boats welcomed the clergy clothed in their vestments and bearing lit candles. They were followed by small boats built by the bourgeois. Hymns resounded on the river while all the bell-towers chimed. The "water pageant", accompanied by the crowd along the quays, proceeded to the Ainay Abbey where - it was thought! - the ashes of the martyrs of 177 were kept. Then, the people climbed up to the St-Nizier et des Saints Apôtres church to revere the relics.

Evening was coming to a close. The pilgrims reached the Pierre bridge, located very near the bridge

The Miniatures Palace, rue Saint-Jean : a sight worth seeing.

bearing the name of Marshal Juin. In front of them were cows and bulls which they prodded along and then... forced into the Saône; the hapless animals tried to swim back to the bank. But when they reached it, the frenzied crowd slit their throats. After this sad exploit, the Festival of the Merveilles, which has become a pagan festival, ended up in the public-houses...

The festival was abolished in the 14th century... "due to excessive swilling, debauchery and paganism...", which, for a religious feast, was stretching things a bit too far!

On September 8th 1643, in order to halt a plague epidemic, the town magistrates vowed to climb up to Fourvière every year, where there was only a modest chapel, in order to offer the Virgin Mary "seven pounds of white wax in candles or in torches and one gold crown..., in order to entreat her to take the city under her special protection". Since this time, on September 8th, when Catholics celebrate the Nativity of the Virgin Mary, the municipality has kept this tradition alive. But all of our city officials do not make the pilgrimage, carrying the gold coin and the wax; they send a delegation and the pilgrimage is carried out... in cars. Some wits even claim that this climb up to Fourvière finishes up merrily in a Lyon "bouchon" (a small, family-owned restaurant, serving dishes specific to Lyon and the surrounding region)! But this must surely be shameless slander!

Since we are speaking about the colours of Lyon in this book, how can we not speak about the most brilliant festival in our city: the one celebrated on December 8th when Christians celebrate the Immaculate Conception and Lyon citizens celebrate one of their most popular traditions.

In 1851 - twenty years before the Bossan Basilica was built, the bell-tower of the ancient Fourvière chapel had been "modernized", in order to place atop it a gold-plated Virgin Mary created by the sculptor Fabicsh. The inauguration was to take place on September 8th, 1852. But the workshop where the statue had been stored was invaded by the swelling

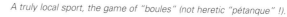
A truly local sport, the game of "boules" (not heretic "pétanque" !).

*The watermen of our «two rivers» have their own chapel,
their own chaplain and their own pardon.*

*Previous page :
in a barge, the watermen's chapel.*

waters of the Saône: the ceremony had to be put off until December 8th.

On that day, Cardinal de Bonald blessed the gold-plated Virgin Mary, who, since that time has towered above the city. Bells pealed, the garrison's guns roared, the nearby streets rang out with hymns... In the evening, the new bell-tower and the lovely statue were to be lit up, but the rain and storm unleashed their fury on the torches, the "Bengal" fireworks and the candles: once again, the illumination had to be put off.

A few hours later, the wind dropped and the rain stopped. Then, all together and as if by instinct, the people of Lyon started placing small candle-ends on their windows. Thousands of will-o'-the-wisps flickered on the quays and then in the public squares; they multiplied throughout the streets and became millions of tiny living flames in honor of theVirgin Mary, right to the very backs of dead-end streets and courtyards. It is said that the astounded

This was the origin of our festival of the 8th of December.

Nowadays in Lyon, our churches and public buildings, not to mention our fountains and statues, are floodlit. Gold gleams on the facades. Small flames shine in all the windows. From the cathedral, the stained-glass windows and rosettes, illuminated from within, are ablaze with colour. Ardent Catholics, bearing a candle-end, set off to climb Fourvière up to the lights; they are welcomed in the basilica by the archbishop and pray together in the sanctuary.

This religious festival is now coupled with a lay festival. For some, this is most unfortunate!

On December 8th, the tradesmen start the "fifteen days of Christmas", light up their shops, decorate their shop windows in the most extraordinary ways. In the shining night, between the greasy smoke of sausages being roasted over embers and the sweet aroma of almonds browning in copper kettles, the crowd goes "window-shopping", decides where to stop to eat; beer or Coca-Cola merchants provide drink for those who have not been able to find a place in packed cafés.

It is not before morning that one goes home and blows out the last candle-ends, still alight.

When Pope Jean-Paul II visited the capital of the Gauls, the city was illuminated, as for December 8th. Additionally, in honor of the sovereign pontiff, the municipality set off fireworks, accompanied by the music of Jean-Michel Jarre.

There is another festival which is very famous in Lyon: this one takes place on July 14th. Once again, fireworks light up the sky over Fourvière and cast shifting rainbows over the water of the Saône; here and there on public squares, dances go on late into the night, and one hears waltzes being played on accordions, or the frenzied hammering of rock-bands...

On June 24th, 25th and 26th 1996 the Rhône-Alps capital hosted the G7. Gathered around Jacques Chirac, President of France, were the heads of state and governments of the richest countries in the world...

In this world, where so many children die of hunger, where the starving cry out their despair, where the victims of infectious epidemics die along the roadside, where unemployment is widespread, and, as a result, where misery is pervasive...

Next page : the «Vogue» (fair) moves from one quarter to an other.

92

For the "have's" of the earth, this "involved uniting donations, assistance missions and investments intended to help the poorest countries, coordinating their efforts, fighting together against terrorism, demanding that all countries respect the rights of man to liberty, food, education, well-being..."

Lyon has always known how to assume the role of host. One has only to remember the entry of kings or statesmen between the Rhône and Saône! In order to welcome these notables of this tormented 20th century, the city revived the splendors of the past.

The heads of state, their wives and their associates stayed in the finest hotels. The streets were adorned with numerous flags. One walked about under vaults decorated with the colours of France, Germany or Italy, the Union Jack of the British, under the maple leaf of the Canadians and the rising sun of Japan, under vaults lit up by the stars of the United States and those of Europe!

The squares, "places" and monuments were covered with flowers. Blue and red - the colours of Lyon - were in sharp contrast with the green colours of the lawns or the foliage of the Tête d'Or park, the Place Maréchal Lyautey, the Place Bellecour; between the quays up to the pink or cream-coloured buildings glided the deep blue of the Rhône or the tender green of the sluggish Saône.

During the Pennants festival....

94

*Jousting on the Saône has drawn "bargees" and water sports
fanatics here since the nautical festivities of antiquity...*

The colours of Lyon also exploded in the courtyard of the Conservatoire national supérieur de
musique: the Lyon rose-growers spread out a carpet
of thirty thousand of their most dazzling flowers for
the wives of the heads of state, and the silk-traders
displayed their most luxuriant creations.

When night fell, the city's hosts, accompanied
by the mayor and the city council, admired fireworks
set off in each district at the same time, accompanied by the steady rhythms and multiple colours of
Maurice Ravel's Boléro.

Finally, to close the festivities, the President of the
Republic offered the Lyon citizens an exceptional
fireworks display and musical show! On the Saône
quay, the setting was in front of the Palais de Justice
with spot-lit columns; the proscenium: the bridge
and the Saône: the scenery: the hill, the basilica, the
cathedral, the buildings as if gilded or aglow in the
light of the spotlights. All kinds of music represented

the exploding of bombs, accompanied by "Bengal" fires, those multicoloured pearls which leap up in the sky, or lasers which shot forth their blue arrows. Jazz could be heard as well as symphony music, and then a choir of young people, an opera duet. There were dancers, like golden flowers twirling around on the bridge pursued by acrobats on stilts...

Never had the citizens of Lyon seen such a show, with such enchanting colours!

Nonetheless, we should not forget that these festivals heralded a very serious and generous international meeting. Helping poor countries be a little less poor is a program capable of stirring up enthusiasm!

In any event, whether in the past, during visits from kings, or in order to celebrate major religious occasions, whether for fairs, or for the arrival of the Pope or a summit-meeting such as the G7, the people of Lyon, who are said to be secretive, reserved, always so aloof and concerned about others will say, know how to let their hair down and prove their love for festive occasions and make the colours of Lyon shine forth.

The city and its associations have revived the festivities of the past. This is the Pennants festival.

VIII - The Colours of Lyon on the Painted Walls of the City

Urban transport in the Avenue La Cassagne. By the "Cité de la création".
Next page : the Tony Garnier Urban museum. By the "Cité de la création".
Previous page : the wall of literature. By the "Cité de la création": .

Jean, just three years away from retirement, managed a large department in the prefecture; Irène, his wife, was responsible for an association of private libraries. Their only daughter, Paule, had the dreaded but unavoidable job of tax inspector.

- "I think that I have good insight into the soul of Lyon and a thorough knowledge of its past", she stated.

Irène was only interested in books and their readers, which, after all, is not such a bad thing!

As to Paule, she had just, not without some concealed regrets, celebrated Saint-Catherine; but she abhorred her first name, since, as she said:

- "My friends call me Pépée, which, considering the job I have, is a little irreverent!"

Did Jean know all about Lyon?

Jean, his wife, his daughter and I met one Saturday in May on the Place de la Croix-Rousse in front of the Jacquard statue; Jacquard was the astute engineer who had transformed the weaving loom. From there, we went to the Canute wall. My guests were not familiar with it. There is a stairway between the buildings. A certain number of small plateaus have to be scaled before reaching a retaining wall such as one runs across so often on the slopes of the Plateau. A cyclist was climbing it, lugging his bicycle on his shoulder. A mother and her child paused to catch their breath... Laundry hung out to dry in the window on the fourth floor. On the second floor, Guignol and Madelon were talking, smiling, watched from afar by a mustached gendarme with his hat cocked aslant.

One had to get a few meters closer in order to appreciate the perfection of the trompe-l'oeil style.

- "Fantastic! cried Paule, "This tree is painted with such perfection that one expects to see it lose its leaves and one feels as if one could actually climb the steps behind the cyclist!"

- "The surface is completely flat!" exclaimed her mother.

- "How in the world was one able to imagine and execute such a décor?" wondered Jean. "One has to really look closely in order to distinguish the painted details from reality. The depth of this superb painting is extraordinary! One might have thought that the Croix-Rousse had acquired an additional district!

- "Here there used to be a horrible, bare facade. It was 1 200 square meters long. Fifteen artists, members of the distinguished team called the "Cité de la Création" had decided to use this surface. Each of them tried to come to terms with the meaning of the Croix-Rousse, its past and present life, its aspirations and dreams. Little by little, images were created in the mind of each artist. The drawings were set off against each other. A synthesis of all the coloured ideas brought the different points of view together. This trompe-l'oeil style, more true-to-life than nature, was then executed and the dream became reality.

- "Yes of course," Irène admitted, "But how did the painters manage make the distinctions between pictures and reality - between what is true and what is imaginary - almost indistinguishable?"

- "That is only a question of technique, of knowing how to implement perspectives, precise proportions, shadows which are clearly delineated or

blurred together, of choosing just the right colours. Then, it was merely up to the individual artists to work with their paintbrushes, the sweat of their brows and sheer force, and so forth. It should be remembered that this is the largest trompe-l'oeil in Europe. Last month, a German claimed that with this décor, Lyon had acquired an additional monument.

Four pigeons with slate-gray wings, green and mauve-coloured necks started pecking on the ground just in front of us. The sound of a car motor frightened them away.

Pépée had forgotten the piles of declarations that she would have to deal with when she got back to her office; she too was entranced by the décor rising up in front of us.

Irène, the librarian, was daydreaming before this magnificent wall, so alive, so colourful:

- "The personages in this painting," she said, "are not very numerous, but their gestures remind us of everyday things; a dog is waiting for his master on a terrace; a tomcat is frisking about on the steps, another one high up on a roof, is eyeing the pigeons; Guignol, Madelon, the mustached Gendarme and the sign "Au rendez-vous des Gônes" sum up the commonplace life of this 'village' which is so heart-warming and which will remain as long as possible - at least, that's what we hope! - this little corner of the Croix-Rousse."

My visitors were familiar with the Giant Pebble, the Boulevard, a few of the alleys; the Canute

Some of Lyon's famous characters, quai Saint-Vincent, in a grand mural fresco by the "Cité de la création".

The "Wall of Life", in the Grange-Blanche quarter.
By the "Cité de la création".

museum no longer held any secrets for them - at least that is what they said - since madam had purchased a silk tie there for her husband and a scarf for her daughter. Her husband had purchased an ancient beer-bottle with a stopper, which he intended to use to decorate his living-room wall with.

Walking along the Grand rue, we entered the curious Rosa-Mir garden. A Spanish mason had created it all by hand; he dreamed of an enchanted place, and drew lanes and clumps of flowers there, built trellises, columns and balustrades; he mixed gravel with shells and cut the stone; then he grew multicoloured flowers, shrubs which were forever green and vines. He dedicated this work, which had taken such a long time, to his mother. When Senis Mir died in 1983, the city took charge of this "extraordinary garden", as Charles Treynet would call it if he were familiar with it!

Paule spoke:

- "This garden makes one think, however modestly, of the perfect Palais d'idéal d'Hauterives which a famous postman called Cheval had built. Like him, this Spaniard was obsessed by a dream; images took shape in his mind and then he set cou-

102

rageously to work. Ultimately, his dream developed into a fabulous reality!

- "There are other painted walls in the city. And all take Lyon as their subject," I added.

We had reached the Place Fousseret, on the right bank of the Saône.

Above the glacier which is so well-known to the people of Lyon today, as in the past, there is a wall painting representing the Cour des Loges. A theater curtain unfolds. Then the patio appears, set out between four Renaissance buildings, comprising the lobby of this luxury hotel frequented by dignitaries from around the world.

In the Avenue Lacassagne in the 3rd district, there is a marvelous fresco which constitutes an authentic outdoor museum.... Seven paintings extend over 120 meters in length with, as the main inspiration, a century of public transport... They cover the years since the first funicular railway up to the Bus-Metro-High-speed Train connection. In the mind's eye, various types of vehicles transport visitors across the Saint-Georges district (at the end of the 19th century), the Croix-Rousse in 1900, the Gerland Universal Fair in 1916, the "1930's" in Perrache, the Terreaux at time of the Liberation, the La Duchère structures, the futuristic Part-Dieu center. (Walls which were also painted by the Cité de la Création).

Here one admires one of the last stagecoaches on the Saône quay, with ladies in crinoline and men in formal dress. On the Place Bellecour, a horse-drawn vehicle is parked. In the puppet theater, Guignol, a Gendarme and Gnafron try to push the broken-down "Guillotine". In 1930, this picturesque steam engine, always decorated with an acid, black smoke, still pulled five or six passenger wagons between Lyon and Neuville. It was said that it had decapitated an unfortunate pedestrian who had fallen onto its track - which is how it got its name!

Further on are paintings of the first solid-tire buses: they linked Gerland from the Place Sathonay. In most districts in the city, one can find various types of tramways, buses, trolley buses, and later, the underground...

All these paintings are teeming with life and constitute a complete inventory of the various means of locomotion!

The colours are authentic, vivid. Dark colours would have been melancholic.

Our companions are most strange! When there is no sunshine, they are down in the dumps! Too

The Silk-Weaver's Wall in the Croix-Rousse. By the "Cité de la création".

much sunshine and they feel dizzy! A moon-less night makes them think of death! And the full moon makes them romantic!

The "wall of life" is erected at the corner of the Rue Feuillat... not far from the Edouard Herriot hospital, which was considered to be so modern.... just a short while ago! A luminous sky changes from marine blue, to light blue, and then to an ethereal milky white. It shelters the Lyon "Olympus" gods of health. Gathered around François Rabelais, the immortal ancestor who lived in the 16th century, are Charles Pravaz, Claude Bernard, Léopold Ollier, Mathieu Jaboulay. Later, Léon Bérard, Alexander Laccassagne, René Leriche, Louis Paufique, Paul Santy and many others were added to this empyrean. Near these masters were the disciples of Aesculapius who were invited to the Elysian Fields of science - these included gifted research scientists:

the Lumière brothers, Mérieux, Lépine, and others.

These celebrities now include: Germain Soufflot who, in the 18th century, transformed and decorated the old Hôtel-Dieu of the Rhône Bridge so splendidly, and Tony Garnier who, in the 20th century, designed an ultra-modern hospital on the Grange Blanche site.

A silhouette of the human body constitutes the symbol of life which, assisted by scholars and doctors, flows in our arteries, our veins, our nerves, our cells. This silhouette is encompassed by a perfectly even cardiogram, a sign of good health.

One should not forget what the world, France and the region all owe to the Lyon school of medicine.

The evening... which had ended by "descending on the plain" between the Croix-Rousse plateau and the Fourvière hill. The thick fog of the Rhône arose and reached the Saône and its valley; Jean, head of a division at the Prefecture, Irène the librarian and their daughter began to feel hunger pangs and their stiff muscles.

They wanted to dine in a Lyon "bouchon", so we went to the " Fédérations" restaurant, in the famous Rue Major Martin. Roses meters long hung from the ceiling, adding their fragrance to the counter where the Morgon wine flowed. The patron recounted his anecdotes, accompanied by the smile of his charming waitresses. He seated us at a table which was often occupied by the Mayor of Lyon and his select circle of guests. We then tasted the Lyon cold pork-meat, liberally basted, and the poultry-liver pastry now known and appreciated throughout the world.

- "Elsewhere, one gobbles down one's food!" I said, "But here, each mouthful must leave an unforgettable souvenir on the taste-buds. The mere sound of chewing, however discreet it may be, is enough to rouse the most sluggish stomach!"

In our "bouchons", wine makes one lick one's chops, then one slowly chews the precious victuals; one savors them, one tastes them... and real connoisseurs then dream of Brillat-Savarin, Curnonsky, Clos-Jouve, André Mure and all our modern specialists of the goddess of Gastronomy and its temples, the "bouchons"!

- "But, in fact", asked Irène, while chewing her "groins d'âne" salad (1)", what do you mean by a `bouchon'?"

- "In the past," I replied, " caterers - inn-keepers and publicans hung a bundle of tightly-bunched straw under their sign: they thus wanted to let the horsemen and coachmen know that they could eat here, rub down ("bouchonner") their horses, dry their sweat, and shine their coats! The word 'bouchon' later assumed the noble meaning that we know today. This means a restaurant with an often modest exterior and a friendly welcome. It must have not a 'bar' - this is not America! - but a 'counter': one counts the jars there; and one speaks about the latestgossip from the area or - if it came to that! - from the city. Politics and love stories are forbidden. It is necessary for guests to be able to see the stove; if there is no kitchen opening onto the dining room, then it is not an authentic bouchon! Formerly, women hustled and bustled about their tin-plated copper pots and concocted precious recipes. They had their celebrities, such as the Dames Filloux or Brazier: they have become the Lyon museums of the gastronomic paradise. Their descendants are called the "Mères". Among us, you will hear one speak about 'mère Brigitte, 'mère Arlette', 'mère Marcelle' - called 'the Great'!), the three 'mères' ending in "Ine", Aline Martine, Evelyne, and so on. Alas, they are less and less numerous, and the men, who are not always "Pères" have supplanted them. One goes to chez Raymond, where we are now. But we could have been welcomed chez Georges, chez Paul, chez Sylvain, chez Nesme and many others! As a chronicler has quite rightly pointed out: "The Lyon Bouchon is neither a bistrot nor a restaurant... but both at the same time!"

It was late! Without going further into the "geste de la gueule", as Rabelais put it, we left the "blissful place of our fortifying feasts".

Since we are speaking about the colours of Lyon in this book, let us point out that the third-largest river in this city had turned the faces of my visitors somewhat red. In the blue night, barely illuminated by a few poorly-lit shop-windows, they went straight to the "Hôtel des Terreaux" in the Rue Lanterne (which had been extinguished for two centuries!). They were then able to enjoy a restful night's sleep, allowing the muscles in their legs and their stomachs to relax in preparation for a tomorrow which promised other delightful adventures.

1 (Foreigners, "who are not like us" speak of "dents de lion" and Parisians - always so well-informed!!! - refer to "pissenlits" (dandelions).)

A Picture book Story of Lyon

IX - A Picture-book Story of Lyon

A futuristic view of the new Place du Pont .

Early the next morning, I found my friends on the terrace on the roof of their hotel.

From this marvelous belvedere, Fourvière, its basilica, its metal tower and the foliage of its gardens, seemed to be concealed, as out of modesty, in the pastel pink of the morning. The silvery Saône, barely awake, slid slowly between the greenery of its banks. Elsewhere, on the quays, cars were already proceeding full steam ahead with their daily rally.

- "Today, we are going to the United States!" I cried.

And, as they seemed startled, I added:

- "Rest assured! I am only referring to a district in

The "Halle Tony Garnier".

our city which took this name when the Americans entered the war on our side in 1918."

We drove along the Rhône quay. I then explained to my friends the reasons why I was taking them to the faraway south-eastern part of the city.

- "The Tony Garnier urban museum, built in the first thirty years of the century, is located in this district. This ingenious architect was well-known before the war of 1914 for his project for an "Industrial City" intended for the benefit of workers, in their factories and homes. He built the Edouard Herriot hospital, numerous villas, World War I memorials, the Gerland stadium, the slaughterhouses, of which only the cattle hall remains.

- "I know that," said Paule, "I saw a show there - 'Notre-Dame de Paris', put on by J.P. Lucet and the Célestin theater!"

We left the Avenue Berthelot and took the Boulevard des Etats-Unis. The weather was nice; sprays of water gushed up from the fountain in the light which made them glimmer with the colours of the rainbow.

- "All these buildings seem new!" cried Irène.

- "Not at all," I answered."They were completed by Tony Garnier in 1933. For him, this meant offering the less-fortunate population low-income flats, which, nonetheless, had facilities which were still rare at that time, not to mention pleasant surroundings."

We walked along the streets. My friends then discovered the walls painted over their entire surface by the artists of the Cité de la Création, whose Canute wall they had admired so much in Croix-Rousse. Some of them included enlarged drawings of the clever architect: the industrial city is painted in light ochre, like the hospital; athletes were running in front of the stadium; cattle were lined up under the steel vault of the large hall; various personalities congratulate the person responsible for this: Herriot, the Lumière brothers, the prefect, while the on-duty photographer installs his equipment; further on, in the atrium of an extraordinary villa, a woman is seated at the foot of a cypress...

- "It has been quite rightly pointed out that his large paintings scattered throughout the district, are like "an open book whose pages one had forgotten to attach" 1.

- "What a remarkable idea!" said Jean, "This urban museum leaves one flabbergasted! It really is... quite extraordinary!"

- "So much so," I added, "that UNESCO sponsors the painters' work: they have adorned the walls with pictures which, without them, would be distressingly bare; they induce people whose life is often difficult, to dream, to aspire to a little beauty and light!"

In order to express themselves just nearby, foreign artists have joined their French comrades.

The Ruse Chestakov group fresco, close up against the others, with small houses, churches, bell-towers with onion-shaped domes, the gates of the city. There is a river with deep blue water. An infinite

number of small green trees has taken over the slightest open space. One might say that this shimmering work was carried out using a child's set of building blocks, imported from the banks of the Volga.

Further on we see Anubis, the jackal-headed god, the red eyeball of Râ, the sun, the eye looking out on the eternity of the pharaoh, two colossuses, brothers to those of Abu-Simbel; the colours are warm: this is the work of Ab Salam Eïd, an Egyptian. Youssouf Bath was inspired by his native Africa. The American Mullican created a group of very modern abstractions...

- "In a word," said Paule, "these painters have decorated these buildings; but, in addition, I think, they also wanted to symbolize the brotherhood which should unite the worlds of artists and manual laborers!"

A magnificent venu for entertainment, the "Halle Tony Garnier" (1913).

112

- "What's more," said her mother, "as you have just said, without its colourful pictures, these walls must have been quite sad; and, if this outdoor urban museum did not exist, do you think that the tenants of these low-rent, state-owned buildings would have taken the trouble to go see the Palais des Arts in your Place des Terreaux? A few of them perhaps! But not all, surely! Thus, one has given them drawings, colours, and life - that is, art right on their own houses. How could they go through their district without opening their eyes?"

On scheduled dates, the tourist board even organizes guided tours through this district which, without its painted walls, would hardly attract many curious visitors. And what is indeed strange, since the completion of these works of art, no scribbling, no signatures of hopeless dropouts, no pseudo-hieroglyphs sprayed on with aerosol cans, no graffiti insulting for society... has bespattered the work of the artists of the Cité de la Création!"

This is the reply of the 'taggers' to a television journalist: "These wall-painters, they do the same job as us!".

This comical reply doubtless hid a desire to return to what is beautiful and a respect for art with realistic pictures and bright colours.

Don't miss your TGV ! (Clock at the Part-Dieu railway station).

In the afternoon, I led my visitors along Rue de la Martinière to the fresco of the people of Lyon at the corner of the St-Vincent quay. Over the 800 square meters of a facade, formerly bare and without the slightest opening, the artists of the Cité de la Création" (them again!) painted 42 windows with curtains, venetian blinds, awnings, balustrades, over six floors. On the ground floor, Bernard Pivot is just coming out of a book shop. Father Pierre and the football player Bernard Lacombe are entering the building. In the nearby bouchon, Paul Bocuse is preparing a meal for Frédéric Dard who, while waiting, samples the Beaujolais wine, and so forth.

On the 4th floor, as in a modern Saint Irenaeus empyrean, the second Bishop of Lyon appears next to Sainte Blandine, the young slave martyred in 177.

On the 3rd floor, the poetess Louise Labbé is speaking with Maurice Scéve: these are two of our most famous Renaissance personalities. Madame Récamier is dreaming on her balcony, doubtless of her friend Chateaubriand. Then comes Bourgelat, who founded the first veterinary school in Lyon, under Louis XV. Pauline Jaricot, creator of the Propagation de la Foi, is next to Sainte Claudine Thévenet, so dear to Cardinal Decoutray.

On the 2nd floor, we see Major Martin whose fortune building was given to Lyon, enabling one to found a school for children from poor families, the economist Jean-Baptiste Say, the physicist Ampère, Laurent Mourguet, the father of Guignol, Saint-Exupéry, the extraordinary aviator novelist...

On the first floor are Antoine de Jussieu, the botanist, Marcel Mérieux, the chemist who believed in Pasteur, Claude Bernard, the professor of medicine. Herriot is speaking with Tony Garnier; the Lumière brothers are discussing films and photography.

On the back facade of the Saint-Vincent quay, there are twelve open windows facing the Saône. The Emperor Claudius -who was born in Lyon - is looking at the hill where the Roman city was founded. Just next to him, the crow-god Lug, worshipped by the Gauls, spreads his wings opposite the city which took its name from him: Lugdunum (city of the god Lug).

Puvis de Chavannes, who decorated the grand stairway of the Palais des Arts, has just completed a new work. Next to him, the explorer Verrazan is gazing at the far-off horizon which he discovered beyond the Hudson river, toward French Canada.

On the ground floor, Philippe de la Salle, to

whom we owe marvelous brocades, and Jacquard, the engineer who was to transform the weaving loom, are waving to us.

- "Here," said Irène the librarian, "is the essential part of the history of Lyon. When looking at these personages, how can one not want to know more, rush into a book-shop, read about the authors, the artists and their work covering the Lyon region?"

My friends left the city, their minds full of pictures and their hearts gladdened, they told me kindly.

The urban museum is an exceptional idea. Since, behind these artistic ordeals, in the background, one sees the events of everyday life, engraved for eternity. Today, at the foot of the walls, children play basketball; they hear the brisk steps of passers-by, the whispering of people visiting a museum that one neither opens nor closes, and that is not guarded. There are the inhabitants of the city, who, like robots, walk along all these streets which have been transformed into imaginary art galleries.

Aline Duret (Murs peints, published by Créations du Pélican, 1994)

The Rhône Banks Park, in Gerland:
declining the future with open spaces and relaxation.

In the Transfigured
Night !

X - In the transfigured night !

The old yrllow stone Forts wake up at night under the spot-lights.

For several years, following the examples of capitals and other major European cities, the city decided to illuminate its monuments and numerous urban sites, as of nightfall.

Thus, the Notre-Dame de Fourvière Basilica, the St-Jean Cathedral and our loveliest churches have come out of the pale light, which does not always fill the Lyon sky!

The metal tower which, by day, is not particularly beautiful, takes on the allure of sapphire lace by night.

The twenty-four columns of the Palais de Justice rise up like a pseudo-antique scene on the bank of the Saône. In Bellecour, the bronze statue of Louis XIV and his horse, the two Coustou statues shimmer in lustrous bronze, under the light of the spotlights. At night, the chestnut trees retain the new green colour of their springtime leaves, throughout the year.

On the Place Antonin Poncet, the bell-tower of the former Hospice de la Charité rises up in front of the Post Office like a candle, reminding one of the charitable work of the Aumône Générale (poorhouse), created in the 14th century. On the lawn, the water and light of a vast fountain play out their elegant games...

The quays, the bridges, the lit-up footbridges sketch colourful rainbows on the rivers.

Electricity restores to the Town Hall all the classical glory of the works of Mansard; our opera, lovelier by night than by day, turns crimson every evening!

The university buildings reflected on the waters of the Rhône.

121

The streets of the old districts, the thoroughfares of the peninsula, the avenues the east of Lyon and their shop windows remain lit up until morning.

The light plays in the foliage of "Pierre Scize". "It looks like a fairy garden", a young girl told me one summer evening. And the old stones of the St-Jean fort in Vaise take on the colour of the castles of the Azergues valley, or the churches in the Beaujolais region assume the colours of golden sandstone.

One of the splendid boats of the Naviguinter company glides along the Saône with its decks illuminated as the music of its orchestra dances on the river...

The city is transfigured by the night: it is not really possible to appreciate Lyon without its lighting.

This is why the tourist board organizes after-dinner trips, tourist rides in buses, mini-cruises...

Thus, the tourists rush along, numerous in the Lyon night, as they do during the day, in our old dis-

Previous page : the Renaissance tower of the Gadagne museum.

Saint-Georges foot-bridge.

The hôtel-Dieu seen from the Rhône Bridge.

tricts, in our broad avenues, in the peninsula, in the modernistic urban creations of the Part-Dieu or Gerland, in our museums.

Almost everyone in Lyon is proud of their city on the Rhône; one speaks readily of this pride, sometimes even with a tinge of chauvinism. However, one would have to be something of a philistine or an exiled "Danube peasant" to dare prefer Lyon to Paris, which is undeniably the most prestigious capital in the world.

In the 19th century, the Prefect Haussmann turned Paris into a modern city with wide, gas-lit avenues. At the same time, the Prefect Vaisse modernized the Rue Impériale (of the Republic), the Rue Imperatrice (Pt Herriot), and others. These two great civil servants of the imperial administration proved to be town-planners at a time when this word did not even exist. Each of them understood that light was necessary at night in cities, and strove to generalize the use of gas lighting, thus creating that picturesque historical personage: the street-lamp lighter.

The 20th century which is now drawing to an end, will, thanks to the electricity sprite and its help, have electric arcs, neon lights, spotlights, projectors... for the general betterment of cities, and especially the town founded 2 000 years ago by a certain Munacius Plancus on behalf of several veterans of the Roman legions who were lost on the hill of the god Lug which overlooks the river from Arar to the sluggish waters; this ever-so-attractive Lyon which has become the main city of the Rhône-Alps region and the twin-city of Birmingham, Frankfort, Milan, Barcelona, and still others!

Golden light of the Higher Academy of music setting the Saône alight.

125

A violinist who knew Stravinski and Messiar, and who had worked on the "Domaine musical" with Boulez, came to Lyon and played the Brahms concerto in solo.

After his concert, he roamed about the city until two in the morning. The next day, he told a reporter from the "Progrès":

"I wanted to relax. A concert is so tiring for a soloist!

"Almost no more cars on the Saône quay. Almost total silence. The river glides along, asleep under the gently-swaying Saint-Vincent footbridge...

"The light sings in me: then, there springs forth softly in my mind, like the tenderness of a caress of long ago, like a discreetly obsessive harmony, the septet that Arnold Schönberg entitled, 'Night Transfigured'."

What a splendid picture of Lyon and its lights!

Enchanting illuminations on the 8th of December.

Bibliography

AUDIN - *Lyon, miroir de Rome dans les Gaules*, Ed. Fayard, 1965

BIDEAU D. - *Lyon sera détruite*, Ed. de la Taillanderie, 1988

BOURGEOIS L. - *Quand la cour de France vivait à Lyon*, Ed. Fayard, 1980

CHAUVY G. - *Lyon 40-44 ; Lyon des années bleues ;*
        Histoire secrète de l'occupation, Ed. Plon

CHAUVY G. - *Lyon, le Lyonnais et sa ville*, Ed. La Taillanderie, 1996

DEVOS M.-A. et GAMBIER G. - *Lyon d'art et d'histoire*, La Taillanderie, 1996

DURET A.-L. - *Les Murs peints*, Ed. Création du Pélican

ESCOT chanoine J. - *Fourvière à travers les siècles*, Ed. Lescuyer, 1954

ETEVENAUX J. - *Les Grandes Heures de Lyon*, Perrin, 1992

ETEVENAUX J. - *La Cuisine lyonnaise*, La Taillanderie, 1996

GRISON P. et LECOQ Ph. - *Les Bouchons d'hier et d'aujourd'hui*, article *Progrès* 1994

HERRIOT E. - *Lyon n'est plus*, 4 vol., Ed. Hachette, 1937

LEGRAND P.-E. - *Plus de 30 pièces pour Guignol*

MEYNARD L. - *Dictionnaire de Lyonnaiseries*, Réédité Honoré, 1982

PETIT CROIX-ROUSSIEN - Article d'avril 58 sur le Gros Caillou

RAPIN G. - *La Croix-Rousse à travers l'histoire*, 1986 ; *Chroniques croix-roussiennes*, 1987

ROCHEIX P. - *Histoire de l'hôtel de ville de Lyon*, 1963

RUDE F. - *Le Mouvement ouvrier à Lyon de 1827 à 1832*, Domat, 1945

VITAL DE Valous - *Les Anciens Hôtels de ville de Lyon*, 1882

Achevé d'imprimer septembre 1998
Dépôt légal 3e trimestre 1998
IMPRIME EN UE